UTRECHT

TRAVEL GUIDE

2023

The Ultimate Guide to exploring a city in Netherland: Discover the culture and explore the great sights and hidden gems of Utrecht

Christopher Levell

Copyright

TABLE OF CONTENTS

25

1.INTRODUCTION

About This Guide

This is the Utrecht Travel Guide for the year 2023. Whether you are a seasoned traveller or a first-time visitor, this guide will help you learn about the charming city of Utrecht. This book will help you organise a fantastic vacation to one of the Netherlands' most alluring locations since it is filled with important details, insider advice, and suggestions.

Welcome To Utrecht

The bustling and ancient city of Utrecht, which is located in the centre of the Netherlands, provides a special fusion of traditional charm and contemporary vitality. You'll be welcomed by a cheerful environment as soon as you enter Utrecht, where charming canals, gorgeous architecture, and kind residents combine to produce an amazing experience.

Utrecht At A Glance

The Netherlands' fourth-largest city, Utrecht, is renowned for its illustrious past, rich cultural legacy, and vibrant intellectual scene. The renowned Dom Tower, the largest church tower in the nation and a representation of the city of Utrecht, is located there. Utrecht is a must-visit location for tourists because of its intact mediaeval city centre and plenty of historical landmarks, museums, and exciting cultural events.

Utrecht is sometimes referred to as the "City of Bicycles" because of its enormous network of bike lanes and the locals' predilection for this environmentally beneficial means of transportation. Due to its small size, the city is perfect for touring on foot or by bike, enabling tourists to take their time and find hidden jewels, attractive neighbourhoods, and delicious cafés.

Utrecht's History and Culture

Over 2,000 years of intriguing history may be found in Utrecht. It was established in 47 AD by the Romans and immediately became a major hub for commerce and religious influence. The name of the city comes from a Roman fort called "Traiectum," which means "fordable crossing" and alludes to a place where the Rhine River could be bridged.

Utrecht prospered as a centre of religion and culture throughout the ages. With the building of the magnificent Dom Church and the accompanying ecclesiastical monuments, it became the centre of religion for the northern

Netherlands throughout the Middle Ages. The city drew pilgrims from near and far due to its religious importance, leaving a lasting impression on its architectural and cultural legacy.

Due to its substantial student population and robust artistic sector, Utrecht has a dynamic and diversified cultural environment. The city presents a broad variety of creative disciplines via some festivals, exhibits, and performances held throughout the year. Music lovers from all over the world come to the Utrecht Early Music Festival, one of the most well-known occasions of its type.

Utrecht has embraced modernism recently while yet maintaining its traditional charm. Formerly industrial districts of the city have experienced urban regeneration, becoming thriving cultural destinations. The design, fashion, and culinary cultures in Utrecht are thriving, and the city is being revitalised by new ideas and regional projects.

In conclusion, Utrecht provides an alluring blend of modern appeal with history and culture. This guide will assist you in navigating the city's attractions, experiencing its cultural offers, and finding the undiscovered jewels that distinguish Utrecht as a travel destination. So be ready for a tour through Utrecht that will live long in the memory, where centuries of history and a lively present clash to produce a genuinely unique experience.

2. PLANNING YOUR TRIP

Best time to Visit Utrecht

To get the most out of your trip, it's important to choose the ideal time to visit Utrecht. A moderate marine climate characterises Utrecht, with cold winters and warm summers. The city's attractiveness may be appreciated all year round, although several seasons have particular benefits.

In Utrecht, the springtime months of April and May are especially lovely. As flowers blossom, the city comes to life with brilliant colours, and the weather is often pleasant with temperate temperatures. Since Utrecht is conveniently situated next to the famed Keukenhof Gardens, this is also a fantastic time to see the well-known Dutch tulip fields in full bloom.

The months of June through August are the peak tourist season in Utrecht. You may take advantage of extended daylight hours and enjoy the bustling activities in the city's parks, canals, and outdoor patios. However, at this time, be ready for sporadic downpours and heavier people.

Utrecht is most beautiful in the autumn, from September through November. The gardens and tree-lined streets of the city are painted in vivacious shades of red, orange, and gold. Although it is usually comfortable outside, it is always a good idea to pack clothing since the weather may change quickly.

With the chance of snowfall, the winter season, which lasts from December to February, has a special beauty. Cosy cafés, Christmas markets, and seasonal accents in Utrecht provide an ambience. Winter days are shorter than summer days, and the weather might be cold, so bring warm clothes.

How to get to Utrecht

Due to its handy location in the Netherlands' centre, Utrecht is readily accessible by a variety of transportation options.

- **By Air:** Amsterdam Airport Schiphol, 30 kilometres to the west of Utrecht, is the closest international airport. Utrecht can be reached by train in just under 30 minutes from the airport. As an alternative, direct bus connections are also offered.

- **By Train**: With excellent train connections to numerous domestic and foreign locations, Utrecht is a significant Dutch rail hub. With frequent and quick train service, the city is well connected to important cities like Amsterdam, Rotterdam, and The Hague.

- **By Car**: Utrecht is conveniently close to major highways, making it simple to get there by car if you prefer to travel that way. It's crucial to remember that parking in the city centre can be scarce and expensive, so it's best to use park-and-ride facilities or choose public transportation to get around the area.

Getting Around Utrecht

Utrecht is a delight to explore on foot or by bike due to its small size and top-notch infrastructure. You can move through the charming streets and along the picturesque canals with ease and efficiency thanks to the city's well-designed network of cycling paths. In the city, there are several rental businesses where you may hire bicycles.

Utrecht's public transportation system is also effective and practical. The local transportation provider, U-OV, runs a vast network of buses and trams throughout the city. For hassle-free travel, you can buy single tickets or use the OV-chipkaart, a rechargeable smart card. The city's main train station, Utrecht Centraal, serves as a significant transportation hub with connections to local and distant locations.

Travel Tips and Local Etiquette

Although Utrecht is a safe city, it is always advisable to exercise common sense safety precautions like watching your belongings and avoiding isolated or dimly lit areas at night.

Because cycling is very popular in Utrecht, always use the designated pedestrian areas when crossing the street.

It's standard politeness to greet residents with a cheerful "Goedemorgen" (good morning), "Goedemiddag" (good afternoon), or "Goedenavond" (good evening) while entering a store, restaurant, or other public venues.

Tipping is not necessary in the Netherlands, since service costs are frequently included. However, it is traditional to round up the amount or give a little tip as a token of gratitude for excellent service.

Utrecht is a cosmopolitan city, and English is commonly spoken. However, learning a few simple Dutch words, such as "Dank u wel" (thank you) or "Alstublieft" (please), may go a long way in expressing respect for the local language and culture.

By keeping this travel advice and local etiquette in mind, you'll be well-prepared to traverse Utrecht with ease and make the most of your stay. Whether you prefer to explore the city on foot, ride through its streets on a bike, or jump on public transit, Utrecht's charm and warmth will make your vacation an amazing experience.

3. TOP ATTRACTIONS IN UTRECHT

Dom Tower and Dom Square

The Dom Tower, a magnificent Gothic building that dominates the city's skyline, is one of Utrecht's most recognisable sights. It is the highest church tower in the Netherlands, standing at 112 metres. For an incredible panoramic view of Utrecht, visitors may ascend the 465 steps to the summit. The Dom Church and other ancient structures may be seen in the nearby Dom Plaza, which is the biggest plaza in the city. The plaza is a hive of activity and a must-see location in Utrecht since it often hosts events and festivals.

Rietveld Schröder House

Schröder House is a UNESCO World Heritage site, and it is a must-see for design fans. This distinctive home, which was created by the renowned Dutch architect Gerrit Rietveld in 1924 and is an emblem of the De Stijl movement, is distinguished by its minimalist style and use of primary colours. The home serves as a showcase for Rietveld's ideas on the flexibility of space and the fusion of art and architecture. The history of the home and its influence on contemporary design is revealed during guided tours.

Centraal Museum

One of the first municipal museums established in the Netherlands is the Centraal Museum, which is housed in a magnificent mediaeval structure. It has a broad assortment of historical, artistic, and design artefacts. Both current art exhibits and paintings by Dutch masters like Gerard van Honthorst and Joachim Wtewael are available for visitors to see. The museum also has a department devoted to the history and culture of Utrecht, which offers insightful information on the past of the city.

Oudegracht (Old Canal)

A trip to Utrecht would not be complete without taking in the captivating Oudegracht, the city's renowned historic canal. The Oudegracht has a distinctive ambience since it is lined with quaint cafés, shops, and wharf basements. Embark on a boat excursion to see the city from a fresh angle or take a leisurely walk around the riverfront. The Werfkelders (quay cellars), which are cosy restaurants and pubs, are also located along the canal, making it a great place to unwind and take in the atmosphere of Utrecht.

Miffy Museum

The Miffy Museum is a must-see destination for families taking vacations with small children. The popular children's book character developed by Dutch illustrator Dick Bruna served as the inspiration for the museum's interactive and instructive exhibits. Children may play imaginatively, discover Miffy's world, and take part in a variety of art and craft projects. The museum is an excellent family-friendly attraction in Utrecht since it offers a pleasant area for kids to study and have fun.

Botanical Gardens

Explore the tranquilly of the Botanic Gardens at Utrecht University to get away from the city's noise and bustle. This botanical wonderland provides a tranquil escape with more than 6,000 plant species dispersed throughout numerous themed gardens and greenhouses. Discover the many habitats, such as the alpine areas, succulent gardens, and tropical jungles. For visitors of all ages, the gardens often feature transient exhibits, seminars, and guided tours, offering a varied educational experience.

These top Utrecht attractions showcase the city's extensive history, magnificent architecture, artistic riches, and scenic surroundings. Each location, from the imposing Dom Tower to the tranquil Botanic Gardens, offers a distinctive window into Utrecht's cultural past and gives guests life-changing experiences. Your comprehension and enjoyment of this amazing Dutch city will increase as a result of seeing these sights.

4. HIDDEN GEMS AND LOCAL FAVOURITES

1.Museum Speelklok

The Museum Speelklok, a hidden treasure devoted to self-playing musical instruments, lies tucked away in the centre of Utrecht. The museum has a sizable collection of barrel organs, music boxes, and other mechanical instruments. Visitors may take advantage of live performances and hands-on exhibitions where they can discover the enchantment of these musical marvels. Music enthusiasts of all ages may have a distinctive and wonderful experience thanks to the museum's guided tours and special events.

2. Griftpark

Griftpark is a lovely green area that residents like, making it a great place to find calm in the city. This park, which is situated in the attractive Wittevrouwen neighbourhood, has lovely ponds, expansive lawns, and walking paths. It's the ideal location for a tranquil walk or leisurely lunch. Griftpark also has a children's playground, a petting zoo, and a cosy café where you can have a cup of coffee and take in the tranquil scenery. The park is a favourite place for inhabitants to relax and appreciate nature because of its high location, which provides breathtaking views of Utrecht's cityscape.

3. Maliebaan Railway Museum

Fans of history and trains will enjoy a trip to the Maliebaan Railway Museum. The history of the Dutch railroads is shown in this little museum, which is housed in a former station building. It features a wonderful collection of antique railroad artefacts, including locomotives, carriages, and other vehicles. Visitors may tour the exquisitely preserved locomotives, see how the Dutch railway system evolved, and even ride a little steam train. The museum provides a fascinating and nostalgic look back at Utrecht's transportation past.

4. Sonnenborgh Observatory and Astronomy Museum

The Sonnenborgh Observatory and Astronomy Museum, perched atop a stronghold from the

16th century, provides a heavenly experience. Visitors to the observatory may see stars, planets, and other cosmic marvels via a vintage telescope. The corresponding museum offers information on the development of astronomy as well as Utrecht-based scientific achievements. The Sonnenborgh Observatory provides an enthralling voyage through the universe with interactive displays and captivating performances.

Wilhelminapark

Take a break from the bustle of the city and relax at Wilhelminapark. This charming park, which bears the name of Queen Wilhelmina, is a favourite with locals for less, picnics, and outdoor sports. The park has lovely flowerbeds, winding walks, and a delightful pond where you can unwind and take in the view. With its play areas, wide open spaces, and even a small petting zoo, it's a wonderful location for families to relax. The park provides cultural activities during the summer, such as outdoor plays and music festivals.

6. Explore Utrecht's Cafés and Pubs

Visitors must experience Utrecht's thriving café and bar culture by visiting these neighbourhood hangouts. Utrecht has a broad selection of alternatives to suit every taste, from warm brown cafés with their classic ambience to hip coffee shops and craft beer bars. Discover hidden jewels where you may savour a cup of coffee, sip on some local beer, or indulge in delectable Dutch foods by taking a leisurely walk around the city's lovely streets. Two well-liked locations include Café Ledig Erf, a bustling gathering place with a large outside patio, and Café Olivier, a Belgian beer café built in a former church.

These undiscovered jewels and neighbourhood hotspots in Utrecht provide a window into the city's lesser-known attractions and locals' way of life. From the tranquil Wilhelminapark to the enchanted Museum Speelklok, each place offers a unique and unforgettable experience. You'll have a greater understanding of Utrecht's cultural legacy and its lively character by immersing yourself in these regional treasures.

5. UTRECHT'S CULINARY SCENE

1. Must-Try Traditional Dutch Dishes

It is important to experience the local cuisine culture whilst in Utrecht. There are many classic Dutch meals available in Utrecht that are worth eating, and the Netherlands has a rich culinary history.

Stamppot, a hearty comfort meal prepared from mashed potatoes combined with vegetables like kale or sauerkraut, is one famous Dutch cuisine. It often comes with gravy and rookworst, a smoked sausage. Bitterballen, which are fried meatballs stuffed with a flavorful ragout, are another well-known delicacy. In pubs and cafés, they are often offered as a snack or an entrée.

Seafood aficionados should not miss Hollandse Nieuwe, often known as Dutch fresh herring, a typical Dutch delicacy. It is a raw herring fillet that is accompanied by pickles and onions. Holding the herring by the tail, one normally consumes it by taking little nibbles.

Try stroopwafels, a Dutch delight comprised of two thin waffle wafers sandwiched together with a caramel syrup filling if you have a sweet craving. In Utrecht, these delectable delicacies may be obtained in neighbourhood markets and bakeries.

2. Top Eateries and Restaurants

The food scene in Utrecht is thriving, with a wide variety of restaurants and cafés. There is food to suit every taste, whether you like traditional Dutch fare or flavours from across the world.

In a former monastery, Restaurant Karel V provides a gourmet dining experience with a cuisine that is influenced by products that are in season and are obtained locally. A wonderful eating experience is produced by the restaurant's classy environment and excellent service.

Visit Roberto's if you're in the mood for Italian food. This upmarket eatery specialises in meals that are Italian and are made with the best ingredients. Roberto's in the centre of Utrecht gives a genuine sense of Italy, from handmade pasta to wood-fired pizzas.

Check out De Markt for a more relaxed eating experience. Several food kiosks in this busy food hall provide a variety of ethnic cuisines. De Markt offers a wide variety of foods, from fancy burgers to Asian street cuisine. Pick up a dish from the stand of your choice, then sit down to dine in the busy common area.

3. Specialty Food Stores

Utrecht is renowned for its thriving food markets, where residents and guests may find a wide variety of fresh vegetables, regional specialities, and handcrafted goods.

The major market in the city is the Vredenburg Market, which takes place on Wednesdays, Fridays, and Saturdays. A variety of fruits, vegetables, cheeses, meats, and baked items are available here. It's a terrific location to experience local culture and sample some of the best goods the area has to offer.

Don't miss the Farmers Market on Saturdays at Janskerkhof. Local farmers' organic and sustainable goods are featured at this market. The Farmers Market provides a truly farm-to-table experience, with everything from farm-fresh veggies to free-range eggs and gourmet cheeses.

Visit the Food Union for a unique gastronomic experience. This food market, which takes place on Sundays, offers a range of foreign cuisines from food trucks and booths. Taste international cuisines, such as Middle Eastern falafel, Indonesian satay, and Mexican tacos. Additionally often featuring live music, The Food Union fosters a dynamic and joyful ambience.

Discovering the food scene of Utrecht is a pleasant voyage through tastes and customs.

The city provides a broad selection of gastronomic experiences to suit every taste, ranging from traditional Dutch delicacies to foreign cuisines. Utrecht's culinary culture is likely to make an impact, whether you're eating at a fancy restaurant, touring the neighbourhood markets, or indulging in traditional Dutch sweets.

6. SHOPPING IN UTRECHT

1. Utrecht's Shopping Districts

With its wide selection of stores, boutiques, and marketplaces, Utrecht is a city that provides a great shopping experience. Every shopper will discover something in Utrecht, from designer clothing to unusual antique items.

The pedestrianised district in the city centre, which comprises the streets Steenweg, Choorstraat, and Oudegracht, is the centre of Utrecht's retail scene. A variety of well-known worldwide brands, regional boutiques, and speciality shops may be found here. Discover hidden treasures that provide a vast selection of clothing, accessories, household products, and more by exploring the quaint side streets.

One of the biggest indoor retail malls in the Netherlands is the Hoog Catharijne Mall, which is close to Utrecht Centraal Station. Hoog Catharijne is a shopper's paradise with over 150 retailers, including major fashion labels, electronics stores, and department stores. It also has a wide selection of eateries and cafés, making it an easy location to stop and refuel throughout your shopping binge.

The markets in Utrecht are likewise well-known for offering a variety of goods, from apparel and antiques to fresh fruit. The oldest fabric market in the Netherlands is the Lapjesmarkt, which takes place every Saturday on Breedstraat. You may look through a vibrant selection of fabrics, lace, buttons, and other sewing supplies here.

2. Souvenirs and Local Crafts

Utrecht has a wide selection of special and sentimental souvenirs and regional crafts to help you remember your trip.

The Utrechtse Domtoren small model of the famous Dom Tower is a well-liked memento. These well-detailed reproductions serve as unique keepsakes that perfectly represent the skyline of Utrecht. At souvenir stores and visitor information offices, you may find them in a variety of sizes and materials.

Local crafts in Utrecht are a reflection of the city's rich creative legacy. The pottery known as Utrechtse Heuvelrug is a traditional craft that has been handed down through the centuries and is distinguished by its unique blue and white motifs. Search for hand-painted ceramic plates, bowls, and vases, which make lovely and distinctive keepsakes.

Utrecht is home to numerous excellent craftspeople and designers who are interested in modern design and regional handicrafts. Observe locally produced jewellery, pottery, textiles, and accessories at independent shops and concept stores. The original works showcase the artistry and skill of Utrecht's craftspeople.

Visit Utrecht's bookstores if you're a book aficionado. There are several bookshops in the city, and they provide everything from blockbusters to specialised literature. The city has a significant literary legacy. You may find hidden literary gems and older editions at bookstores that specialise in used books.

retail in Utrecht is a joy because it mixes the finest of traditional markets and local crafts with the best of contemporary retail areas. Every tourist will find something they like in Utrecht's eclectic retail environment, whether they are seeking designer apparel, one-of-a-kind trinkets, or creative works. So gather your shopping bags and get ready to explore the busy streets of the city in search of hidden gems.

7. OUTDOOR ACTIVITIES AND NATURE

1. Cycling Routes in and around Utrecht

A network of well-maintained bicycle paths makes Utrecht and the surrounding districts a cyclist's paradise, allowing you to explore the city and its stunning surroundings on two wheels. Cycling is not only a common form of transportation but also a wonderful opportunity to take in the natural beauty of the area.

The "Tour de Maliebaan" is one of Utrecht's most famous bicycle routes. This path leads you along the storied Maliebaan, a street dotted with opulent houses and flanked with trees. You can immerse yourself in Utrecht's rich history and architecture as you bike along this lovely route, passing through attractive parks, canals, and monuments.

The "Utrechtse Heuvelrug" route is strongly suggested for people looking for a long cycling trip. The Utrechtse Heuvelrug National Park, a stunning natural reserve renowned for its woodlands, heathlands, and dunes, is traversed by this magnificent route. The route provides a variety of natural settings, charming towns, and expansive vistas for a completely immersive outdoor experience.

2. Parks and Recreational Areas

There are several parks and recreational spaces in Utrecht where you may get away from the city's bustle and re-establish your connection to nature. These open areas provide places for relaxing strolls, picnics, sporting events, and other recreational activities.

The Wittevrouwen neighbourhood's Griftpark is a well-liked park that attracts both residents and tourists. There are wide lawns, strolling paths, and a lovely pond there. There are also kid-friendly playgrounds, a petting zoo, and a nice café in the park where you can sip coffee and take in the serenity.

Another jewel in Utrecht's park landscape is Wilhelminapark, which bears the name of the late Queen Wilhelmina. This beautifully manicured park has a central pond, meandering walks, and lush flowers. It's the perfect location for a leisurely picnic or tranquil walk. The park holds cultural activities during the summer, such as outdoor theatre productions and concerts.

3. Boat Tours on Utrecht's Canals

It's a great opportunity to see the city from a new angle to cruise the canals of Utrecht. The lovely canals and attractive waterfronts may be seen while gliding along on boat cruises, which are a very special experience.

Take a boat excursion with a guide or hire a pedal-powered vessel to explore the famed Oudegracht (Old Canal) and the nearby waterways. You'll pass under low-arched bridges, see the recognisable wharf basements, and take in expansive views of the city's attractions as you sail down the canals. The narration on boat trips is often informative and offers insights into the history, culture, and architecture of Utrecht.

4. Visits to Local Nature Reserves Overnight

Due to its convenient location, Utrecht is a great starting point for day excursions to neighbouring nature reserves where you can take in the magnificent scenery and engage in outdoor sports.

Just outside of Utrecht, there is a sizable natural reserve called the Hoge Veluwe National Park, which is renowned for its many ecosystems. There are heathlands, dunes, thick woodlands, and a variety of fauna there. You may take your time discovering the park's natural splendour thanks to its extensive network of walking and bicycle routes. Visit the Kröller-Müller Museum, which is housed inside the park and has an excellent collection of contemporary sculptures and art.

The Biesbosch National Park is another neighbouring natural reserve that is worthwhile seeing. This distinctive freshwater tidal lagoon, which can be found in the province of South Holland, is a refuge for birdwatchers, environment lovers, and boaters. Kayak across the park's complex network of canals or go on a boat excursion to see its diverse wildlife and tranquil surroundings.

There are many possibilities to get away from the city and take in the natural beauty of the area thanks to Utrecht's outdoor activities and nature services. There are many outdoor activities available in and around Utrecht, whether you decide to go cycling along gorgeous routes, unwind in the city's parks, take a boat excursion around the canals, or plan a day trip to adjacent nature reserves.

8. UTRECHT'S FESTIVALS AND EVENTS

1. King's Day Celebrations

One of the most widely observed occasions in the Netherlands is King's Day, or Koningsdag, which is celebrated with vivacious celebrations in Utrecht. Every year on April 27, the city transforms into a sea of orange as people assemble to commemorate King Willem-Alexander's birthday.

There are several events for people of all ages taking place on the streets of Utrecht, including lively markets and live music performances. Boats with decorations line the canals, and both residents and tourists dress in orange to display their Dutch patriotism. Participate in the excitement by shopping at the flea markets, eating delectable Dutch fare, or dancing in the city squares to live music.

2. Festival of Early Music in Utrecht

The Utrecht Early Music Festival is a tribute to the city's dedication to conserving and presenting its cultural tradition. Utrecht is known worldwide for its extensive musical heritage. This festival, which takes place every August, draws music lovers from all over the globe who come together to enjoy the wonder of early music.

During the festival, top-notch artists who specialise in music from the Middle Ages, Renaissance, and Baroque eras play at Utrecht's historic buildings, including the Dom Church and the TivoliVredenburg concert Hall. Attend events that explore the complexity and beauty of early music, such as concerts, recitals, and talks. Experience the captivating sounds of harpsichords, lutes, and other historical instruments as they take you back in time to the times of Bach, Mozart, and Handel.

3. Netherlands Film Festival

At the Nederlands Film Festival, an annual celebration of Dutch film held in Utrecht, movie buffs will find enough to love. The festival offers a forum for up-and-coming filmmakers to display their work while showcasing a wide spectrum of Dutch films, from small productions to blockbuster blockbusters.

across the festival, screenings, premieres, and Q&A sessions with directors, actors, and business leaders are held at different locations across the city. Attend film screenings to see the newest works of Dutch cinema, and participate in debates about the craft. The festival also offers seminars, masterclasses, and exhibits, providing chances to discover the art of filmmaking and acquire knowledge about the Dutch film business.

4. Concerts & Cultural Events

A city that lives on culture and innovation, Utrecht offers a busy schedule of performances and cultural events all year long. Every creative preference may be catered to in Utrecht, where there are constantly events taking place ranging from classical music concerts to exhibits of modern art.

One of Utrecht's top musical venues, TivoliVredenburg, presents a variety of performances, from avant-garde electronic music to traditional symphonies. Attending a live concert at TivoliVredenburg is a must for music enthusiasts because of the venue's varied programming, which guarantees that there is something for everyone.

Several cultural events that highlight the city's inventiveness are also held in Utrecht. The Le Guess that? festival, which takes place in November, is a well-known music event that honours performers that push the boundaries of experimental music. This festival provides a distinctive and all-encompassing musical experience with concerts happening in numerous locations across the city.

The Uitfeest, which ushers in Utrecht's cultural season, is another noteworthy occasion. This one-day event offers performances, exhibits, and outdoor concerts all across the city, giving guests a taste of the thriving cultural life in Utrecht.

The festivals and events in Utrecht give you the chance to experience the vibrant atmosphere of the city and its rich cultural history. There is always something fascinating going on in Utrecht, from the boisterous King's Day festivities to the alluring sounds of early music, from the big screen during the Nederlands Film Festival to the varied variety of concerts and cultural events. Make travel arrangements in advance and be ready to be enchanted by the city's festive atmosphere.

9. NIGHTLIFE AND ENTERTAINMENT

1. Hotspots for Bars, clubs, and Nightlife

The nightlife in Utrecht is lively and varied, with a selection of pubs, clubs, and entertainment establishments to satisfy all interests and preferences. Utrecht has plenty to offer whether you're searching for a cosy pub, a buzzing club, or a chic cocktail bar.

Utrecht's nightlife is concentrated in the city centre, where a wide variety of clubs and taverns line the streets. Particularly the Oudegracht, with its crowded waterfront decks and boisterous ambience, is a well-liked neighbourhood for nightlife. Traditional Dutch pubs, hip cocktail bars, and music venues may all be found here.

Utrecht has several breweries and beer pubs where craft beer fans may experience a broad range of locally made beers. Visit places like Oproer Brewery, De Kromme Haring, or Café Olivier, famed for its wide variety of Belgian beers, to explore the thriving beer culture and sample distinctive brews.

There are many clubs and music venues in Utrecht where you may dance the night away. Rock, pop, techno, and jazz are just a few of the live music events that can be found at the famous concert venue TivoliVredenburg. Both local and foreign DJs perform at the well-known electronic music clubs De Helling and WAS.

2. Theatres and other performance spaces

The cultural landscape of Utrecht encompasses more than just music and nightlife, with several theatres and performance spaces providing a variety of creative experiences. There are many ways to pass the time in Utrecht, from theatre plays to dance performances and comedy acts.

The Stadsschouwburg Utrecht is a renowned theatre that hosts a variety of events, including plays, musicals, and dance shows. It is situated in the centre of the city. The theatre presents both national and international shows, giving budding actors and theatre groups a stage.

Theatre Kikker, a tiny theatre that emphasises modern theatre and experimental performances, is another noteworthy location.

Theatre Kikker is renowned for its creative programming, which includes provocative plays that push the limits of conventional theatre.

In addition, Utrecht has several events honouring the performing arts. The boundaries between theatre, dance, and the visual arts are blurred in the cutting-edge contemporary acts presented during the SPRING Performing Arts Festival. Reputable national and international artists come together for this multi-day event, which offers a distinctive and comprehensive cultural experience.

The Comedyhuis Utrecht is the place to go if you like comedy. Regular stand-up comedy performances with both seasoned and rising comics are presented at this comedy club. In a comfortable and private atmosphere, take pleasure in an evening of laughter and entertainment.

In addition to theatres and other performance spaces, Utrecht hosts several festivals and cultural events all year long. Watch for occasions that highlight the city's many cultural offers, such as the Utrecht International Comedy Festival, the Festival of Literature, and the Utrecht International Film Festival.

There is something for everyone in Utrecht's nightlife and entertainment scene, which caters to a wide spectrum of interests. Utrecht has a dynamic and active environment that will keep you engaged and enthralled, whether you're searching for a fun night out in the city's pubs and clubs or wanting to immerse yourself in the world of theatre and performing arts.

10. ACCOMMODATION OPTIONS

1. Best Areas to Stay in Utrecht

There are various places in Utrecht where you may stay that provide easy access to the city's attractions, food choices, and lively environment. When choosing a place to stay in Utrecht, keep the following in mind:

- **City Centre**: Staying in the city centre places you at the centre of the action and gives you quick access to Utrecht's famous landmarks, popular retail areas, and vibrant nightlife. With its abundance of hotels, hostels, and boutique lodgings, the region around the Oudegracht (Old

Canal) and Neude Square is especially well-liked.

- **Museum Quarter**: Consider lodging in the Museum Quarter if you're eager to see Utrecht's vibrant cultural scene. Numerous museums, like the Centraal Museum and the Dick Bruna House, can be found in this region, along with lovely lanes lined with a variety of cafés and eateries. There are a variety of lodging alternatives in this neighbourhood, including bed & breakfasts and boutique hotels.

- **Utrecht Science Park**: Utrecht Science Park is a great place to stay if you're visiting the University of Utrecht or going to conferences or events at the Jaarbeurs Exhibition Centre. It is situated in the eastern section of the city. Public transit is readily available, and the region has a variety of lodging options, including hotels and apartments, that are close to the city centre.

- **Griftpark Area:** North of the city centre, in the Griftpark district, you'll find a calmer, more residential environment. This leafy district is renowned for its lovely park, picturesque streets, and neighbourhood cafés. It's a fantastic option if you want to stay close to the city centre yet want a more laid-back atmosphere.

2. Inns, hotels, and Hostels

To accommodate various interests and budgets, Utrecht provides a range of lodging choices. You can locate accommodations that suit your preferences, whether you're seeking opulent hotels, affordable hostels, or welcoming bed & breakfasts.

Elegant accommodations, first-rate service, and upmarket facilities are all features of Utrecht's luxury hotels. Numerous of these hotels have beautiful city views and are housed in old structures. The Grand Hotel Karel V, renowned for its opulent accommodations and spa amenities, and the Eye Hotel, which mixes contemporary design with a historic setting, are two well-liked options.

There are many hostels and low-cost hotels in Utrecht for travellers on a tight budget. The Stayokay Utrecht Centrum provides budget-friendly individual rooms and dormitory-style lodging close to Neude Square. For those on a tighter budget, the Mother Goose Hotel, a boutique hotel with chic rooms, also provides affordable prices.

Consider booking a bed and breakfast (B&B) while visiting Utrecht if you'd want a more private and intimate experience. B&Bs offer affordable lodging with a unique flair, often run by hospitable locals who may give suggestions and insider knowledge. The city offers a range of B&B choices, from lovely inns to ancient canal homes.

It is advised to make your hotel reservations in advance, particularly during busy travel times and for significant events. Because Utrecht draws tourists all year long, availability may change. When selecting your lodging, take into account aspects like location, facilities, and your budget to guarantee a relaxing and pleasurable stay in Utrecht.

In conclusion, Utrecht has a variety of lodging choices to accommodate various tastes and price ranges. You may stay in one of the many hotels, hostels, or bed & breakfasts in Utrecht, whether you decide to stay in the city centre, the Museum Quarter, or another neighbourhood.

11. PRACTICAL INFORMATION

Emergency Numbers and Healthcare

It's essential to be familiar with Utrecht's emergency phone numbers and medical facilities in case of an emergency. Here are some critical figures and details to bear in mind:

- **Emergency Services**: The Netherlands' national emergency number is 112. Any emergency scenario, including those involving the police, fire, or medical care, may be handled by calling this number. Indicate your location and the emergency's specifics in your call.

- **Hospitals**: Utrecht is home to several hospitals and other healthcare institutions that provide emergency medical care. A significant hospital and academic medical centre in the city is the University Medical Centre Utrecht (UMC Utrecht). Both the Diakonessenhuis Utrecht and the St. Antonius Ziekenhuis Utrecht are recognised hospitals that provide a wide variety of medical treatments.

- **Pharmacy**: In the Netherlands, pharmacies are referred to as "Apotheek." There are many pharmacies in Utrecht where you may buy over-the-counter medicines or fill prescriptions. While most pharmacies are open during normal work hours, some could provide emergency treatments after hours. For further information, check the hours of operation for the pharmacy closest to you or ask you for lodging.

Finances and Exchange of Currency

When visiting Utrecht, it's crucial to understand financial issues. To remember, have the following in mind:

- **Currency**: The euro (€) is the currency used in the Netherlands. It is a good idea to have extra cash on hand for little purchases and unexpected situations. Although credit and debit cards are extensively used in Utrecht, it's always a good idea to have some cash on hand in case a particular establishment doesn't take cards or has a minimum card payment threshold.

- **Automated Teller Machines (ATMs):** The majority of the ATMs in Utrecht accept the most common foreign debit and credit cards. Look for ATMs connected to international payment systems like Visa, Mastercard, or Maestro. You should verify with your bank to confirm any possible costs since certain ATMs may impose transaction fees.

- **Exchange of Currencies:** Utrecht offers several choices for currency exchange. Currency exchange services are provided by banks and "Geldwisselkantoor," or currency exchange offices. Before engaging in a purchase, it is a good idea to examine exchange rates and costs. Exchange offices are often located in well-known tourist locations or at key transit hubs like railway stations.

- **Tipping**: Although not required in the Netherlands, excellent service is appreciated with a tip. In restaurants, it's customary to add a tip that ranges from 5 to 10% of the final bill. If you are pleased with the service you received from tour guides, hotel employees, and taxi drivers, you should tip them.

Regional Customs and Practical Words

Your experience in Utrecht may be improved by learning some key keywords and local traditions. Here are some pointers and expressions to help you get by in the local tongue:

- **Greetings**: In Utrecht, a standard salutation is "Hallo" (Good morning) or "Goedemorgen" (Hello) for greetings before noon. Between midday and roughly six o'clock, "Goedemiddag" (Good afternoon) is used for greetings, while "Goedenavond" (Good evening) is used in the evening. It's customary to say "Dankjewel" (Dutch for "Thank you") or "Tot ziens" (Goodbye) while leaving a store or restaurant.

- **Politeness**: In general, Dutch people are amiable and straightforward in their communication. It's customary to extend a solid handshake and establish eye contact while greeting. Try to be on time for appointments and other planned events; it is appreciated.

- **Language**: Dutch is the official tongue of the Netherlands. Even though many Dutch people are English speakers, it's always nice to learn a few fundamental Dutch words. Here are some keywords and phrases:

Hello: Hallo
I'm grateful. Thankyou (casual), Thankyou (formal).
Yes: Ja
No: Nee
Excuse me, please.
Are you an English speaker? Do you speak English?

- **Etiquette**: When visiting Utrecht, it's crucial to observe the traditions and etiquette of the area. It is traditional to take off your shoes before entering someone's house. It's polite to wait for everyone to be served before beginning to eat while eating out. It's normal to bring a little gift, such as flowers or a bottle of wine when you're welcomed to someone's home.

- **Bicycles**: Utrecht is renowned for its bicycle culture, and on many routes, cyclists enjoy the right-of-way. Keep an eye out for bike lanes, and always look both ways before crossing the street. Make careful you adhere to local traffic laws and store your bike in specified places while renting a bicycle.

You may make sure that your visit to Utrecht runs more smoothly by being acquainted with some useful characteristics of the city. You can communicate with people and move about the city with ease if you respect cultural traditions and are familiar with key terms.

12. UTRECHT TRAVEL ITINERARIES

1.One Day in Utrecht: Highlights and Must-Sees

Even if you just have one day in Utrecht, you can still take in the city's attractions and enchanting ambience The following is a recommended schedule for a day in Utrecht:

- **Morning**:

Visit Utrecht's famous monuments, the Dom Tower and Dom Square, first thing in the morning. For sweeping views of the city, ascend the Dom Tower's 465 steps.

Wander down the Oudegracht (Old Canal) and discover the distinctive stores and wharf basements that border the waterway.
Discover the rich art and history of Utrecht by going to the Centraal Museum, which is close to the Oudegracht.

- **Afternoon**:

Visit one of the numerous inviting cafés or eateries that along the canals for a leisurely meal.
To see Utrecht's picturesque shoreline and ancient structures from a fresh angle, take a boat excursion around the canals.
Discover bustling shopping areas like Steenweg and Voorstraat, where you can discover a mix of independent stores and well-known retailers.

- **Evening:**

Dine at one of Utrecht's best restaurants, which provides a variety of foreign and Dutch cuisine, to indulge in the city's culinary culture.
Visit the famous music venue TivoliVredenburg after supper to take in a live show or concert.
Spend the evening taking part in Utrecht's vibrant nightlife by visiting the clubs and pubs in the city centre.

2. Utrecht Weekend Getaway

If you have a weekend to spend in Utrecht, you may explore the city's attractions in more detail and go beyond the municipal limits. Here is a proposed weekend trip itinerary for Utrecht:

Day 1:

- Visit the Rietveld Schröder House, a UNESCO World Heritage Site and a prime example of De Stijl architecture, to start your day.
- Discover a broad variety of artistic and cultural exhibits by exploring the Museum Quarter and going to the Centraal Museum.
- In one of the inviting cafés or eateries close to Neude Square, take your time eating lunch.
- Spend the day discovering Utrecht's hidden jewels, like the Maliebaan Railway Museum, which showcases the history of Dutch railroads, and the Museum Speelklok, a museum devoted to self-playing musical instruments.

- Take a stroll around Utrecht's lovely neighbourhoods in the evening to find neighbourhood cafés and pubs where you may unwind.

Day 2:

- Visit the Botanic Gardens, which are part of the Utrecht Science Park, early in the day to take in the tranquil greenery and variety of plant types.
- Take a bicycle rental and tour Utrecht's lovely parks and green spaces, such as Griftpark and Wilhelminapark.
- Take a picnic in one of the parks or get something fast to eat at a nearby market.
- To appreciate the area's natural beauty, take a day excursion to one of the surrounding nature preserves, including

the Hoge Veluwe National Park or the Utrechtse Heuvelrug National Park.
- On your return, have dinner at one of Utrecht's well-liked eateries.

3. A Family and Child Trip to Utrecht

With many kid-friendly events and attractions, Utrecht is a city that welcomes families. A proposed schedule for a family vacation to Utrecht is provided below:

Morning:

- The Miffy Museum, a museum in the city centre devoted to well-known children's book characters, is a great place to start your day.
- Visit the Dom Tower and take a tour around the old streets. Climb the tower if

your kids are old enough for a memorable experience.

- At one of the cafés or restaurants with kid-friendly menus, enjoy a family-friendly lunch.

Afternoon:

- Visit the intriguing Railway Museum (Spoorwegmuseum), where children may examine old trains and even ride a toy train.
- Discover the interactive displays at the Sonnenborgh Observatory and Astronomy Museum, where youngsters can learn about the stars and planets.
- Take a boat cruise along the canals to take in the beautiful scenery of Utrecht.

Evening:

- Visit a cosy eatery in the heart of the city for a family supper.
- Attend a play or performance that is appropriate for the whole family at one of Utrecht's theatres, including Theatre Kikker or Stadsschouwburg Utrecht.

4. Examining the Art and Architecture of Utrecht

The rich artistic and architectural legacy of Utrecht is well-known. A recommended route for discovering Utrecht's art and architectural scene is provided below:

Morning:

- Visit the Centraal Museum first thing in the morning. It is home to a sizable collection of artwork and design, including pieces by well-known Dutch artists.

- Visit Utrecht's art galleries, such as the Kunstliefde and the Fotodok, to find exhibits of modern art.
- Take a stroll around the city centre and take in the distinctive architecture, such as the contemporary Rietveld Schröder House and the Gothic-style Dom Tower.

Afternoon:

- Learn about the university's past and its scientific holdings by visiting the Utrecht University Museum, which is housed in the stunning Academy Building.
- Discover hidden jewels and gain knowledge of Utrecht's architectural

history by taking a guided architectural tour.

- Discover the street art and public art that are distributed across the city.

Evening:

- Attend a musical or cultural event at TivoliVredenburg or another music venue in Utrecht.
- Dine in a place that combines modern architecture with delectable cuisine.
- Take a stroll around Utrecht's well-lit streets to wind down your day and take in the city's magnificent architecture at night.

With the help of these travel itineraries, you can customise your trip to Utrecht depending on your interests and the length of your stay. They provide you with a look into the city's varied facets. Utrecht has a wide variety of activities and experiences to make your vacation unforgettable, whether you have a day, a weekend, or longer.

13. ADDITIONAL RESOURCES

1.Useful Websites and Apps

Several helpful websites and applications may improve your experience and provide important information while planning your trip to Utrecht. Here are some sources we advise using:

- Visit Utrecht (www.visit-utrecht.com): The city of Utrecht's official tourist website provides in-depth details on destinations, activities, lodging options, and travel advice.

- The Utrecht City Guide App is a smartphone application that offers a plethora of information about Utrecht, including maps, points of interest, dining options, and events. It's a useful tool for getting about town and finding secret gems.

- You may plan your trips both within and outside of Utrecht by using NS.nl or 9292.nl, websites and mobile applications that provide up-to-date information on train and public transit timetables.

- Users may post reviews and suggestions for Utrecht hotels, restaurants, and activities on the well-known travel website TripAdvisor. It may be a useful tool for locating reputable businesses and undiscovered treasures.

2. Suggested Literature and Maps

Here are some suggested books and maps for touring Utrecht if you like to have tangible materials with you:

- **Dennis Luijer's "Utrecht**: An Interactive Guide to the City" The history, culture, and architecture of Utrecht are discussed in this travel guide. Maps, suggested routes and information on the city's attractions are all included.

- **Cycling Maps**: A cycling map or guidebook that emphasises the area's bike-friendly trails and attractions is a good investment if you're interested in riding about Utrecht and the surrounding locations.

These extra sources will supplement your travel manual and provide you with useful knowledge, advice, and tools to improve your time in Utrecht.

14. CONCLUSION

The alluring city of Utrecht provides a wonderful fusion of its past, present, and future. Utrecht has much to offer every traveller, from its recognisable Dom Tower to its lovely canals and thriving cultural environment. Utrecht will make an impact on you whether you want to explore its historical sites, immerse yourself in the art and architecture, indulge in culinary treats, or just take in the laid-back ambience.

The biggest attractions, undiscovered jewels, neighbourhood favourites, culinary scenes, outdoor activities, festivals, and useful information have all been highlighted in this travel guide's thorough overview of Utrecht. You may tailor your vacation to Utrecht using comprehensive itineraries for various lengths of time and interests.

Plan your travel and accommodations, think about the ideal time to go, and get to know the regional manners and traditions. To improve your experience and make the most of your stay in Utrecht, use the suggested resources, including websites, apps, books, and maps.

Utrecht will enchant you with its beauty and warmth, whether you're a history buff, an art lover, a nature adventurer, or just looking for a special travel experience. So be ready to explore everything that Utrecht has to offer by packing your luggage and getting set for an adventure. Enjoy your trip and make cherished memories in this beautiful city.

Printed in Great Britain
by Amazon

42898408R00056